Thoro'bred TRACTORS

Osprey Colour Series

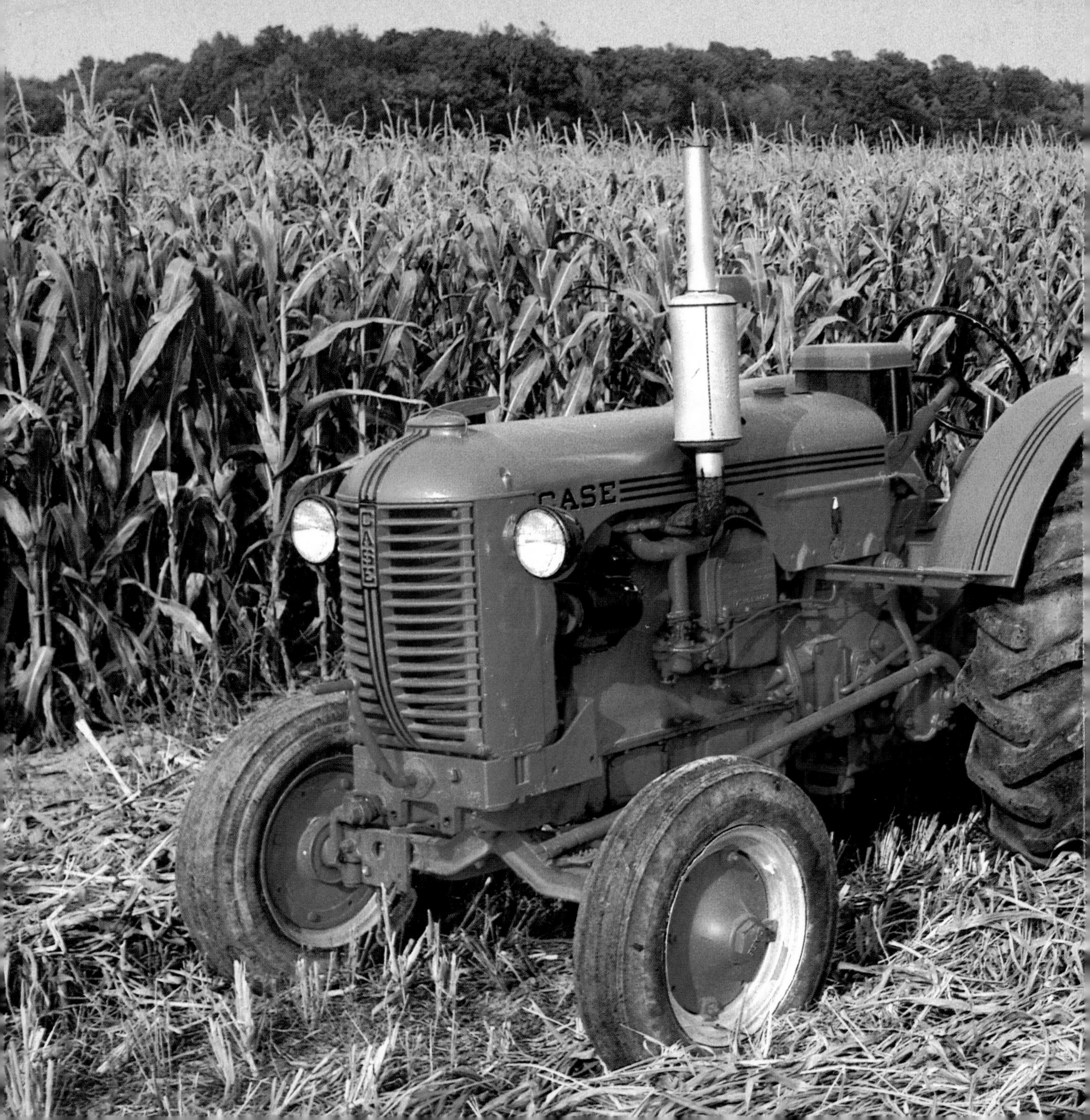

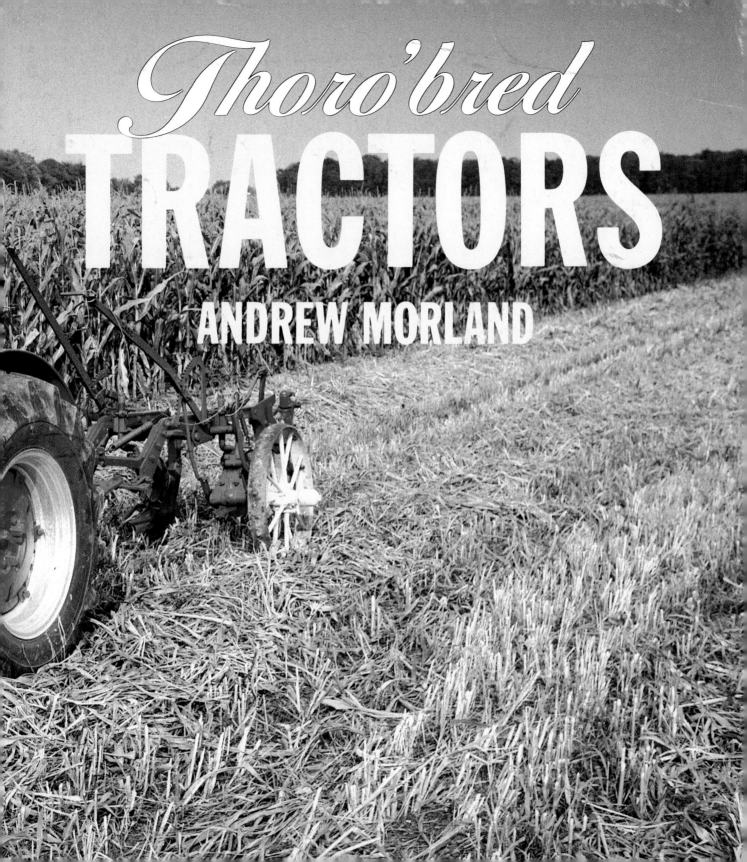

Thoro'bred
TRACTORS

ANDREW MORLAND

Published in 1990 by Osprey Publishing
59 Grosvenor Street, London W1X 9DA

© Copyright Andrew Morland 1990

Editor Nicholas Collins
Designed by Brenda Burley
Printed in Hong Kong

Filmset by Keyspools Ltd,
Golborne Lancashire

British Library Cataloguing in Publication Data
Morland, Andrew
  Thoroughbred tractors.
  1. Agricultural tractors
  I. Title
  629.2'25

ISBN 0-85045-871-4

Front cover illustration

John Deere, for many the epitome of a thoroughbred tractor

Back cover illustration

Henry Ford was passionate throughout his long life about the need to provide farmers with cheap, reliable, and powerful tractors. His ideals were embodied in the Fordson.

Title verso illustration

A Case pictured against the ripening maize in an Iowa field

Contents

Acknowledgements

This book could not have been put together without the help and co-operation of classic farm tractor owners and enthusiasts in North America and Great Britain. Some are named in the text, many are not. Grateful thanks goes to all who made this register of a selection of thoroughbred tractors possible. Thanks are extended especially to the organizers of the farm tractor events covered in this book:

The Prairieville Old Fashioned Farm Days event, held every year over Labor Day weekend at Delton, Michigan, boasts a fine collection of tractors organised by Norman Jahnke. Case steam engines and tractors were shown by members of the JI Case Collectors' Association Inc., Route No. 2, Box 242, Vinton, Ohio 45686-9741.

Another Labor Day weekend event is the Jim Monaghan Antique Engine Show held at Domino's Farms in Ann Arbor, Michigan.

A third Labor Day event is the Western Minnesota Steam Threshers Reunion at Rollag, Minnesota. For readers who wish to make contact, the membership secretary is Janet Briden, PO Box 2162, Fargo, North Dakota 58107, USA.

The Van Buren Flywheelers Antique Engine and Tractor Show at Hartford, Michigan, held over the second weekend in September every year, afforded the opportunity to photograph the locally built 'Friday'.

The North Central Steam and Gas Engine Club of Edgar, Wisconsin has an annual get-together in August at the farm of Kurt Umnus.

Oliver tractors owned by Morrie Pitlick were photographed at the World Ploughing Championships in Iowa.

Ernest Weissert of Bourbon, Indiana, made available his collection of Minneapolis Moline tractors. Tom Graverson of Bremen, Indiana, gave access to his Case collection.

The Dearborn, Michigan-based Henry Ford Museum has a memorable transport collection. One needs more than a day to take in Greenfield Village and the Museum.

In the United Kingdom special thanks must go to the Hunday Museum otherwise known as the National Tractor and Farm Museum at West Side, Newton, Stocksfield-on-Tyne in the north of England. This was started by John Moffitt who collected old tractors from around the world and named his museum after his famous Hunday Friesian herd.

The Great Dorset Steam Fair Limited organizes the Stourpaine Bushes event at the end of August. The Show Secretary can be contacted at the Show Office, Dairy Mead, Child Okeford, Blandford Forum, Dorset DT11 8HD.

The Yeovil Festival of Transport run by Yeovil Car Club in August, provides a gathering ground for tractor enthusiasts.

The South Somerset Agricultural Preservation Club event, Yesterday's Farming, takes place each September. The Club Secretary is Miss S. Moyle, 143 Lower Fairmead Road, Yeovil, Somerset BA1 5SR.

For further information on events and clubs in Great Britain contact the National Vintage Tractor and Engine Club, Brian Sims, 1 Hall Farm Cottages, Church Lane, Swarkestone, Derby DE7 1JB.

For further information on tractor events in the USA and Canada refer to the *Steam and Gas Show Directory*, printed annually by the Stemgas Publishing Company, PO Box 328, Lancaster, Pennsylvania 17603.

Close-up of Case engine and front
grille

Overleaf
Despite its antique appearance, the
Farmall was very modern in terms
of planned maintenance, air and fuel
filtrations plus ease of access to
engine components.

Introduction

Serious attempts at steam-powered ploughing took place in Britain in the 1830s. Although ingenious, the early machinery was too cumbersome to be practical. A more successful steam plough was built in the 1860s, after which steam power was widely adopted. Threshing machines were hauled about the countryside by the new, self-propelled steam traction engines and worked on a contract basis by gangs of labourers. The internal-combustion-engined tractor we recognize today owes its origin to those steam traction engines of the late 19th century.

Many of the tractors pictured in this book can trace their lineage back to the days of steam or shortly thereafter. Hence the title 'Thoroughbred Tractors'. Photojournalist Andrew Morland is the author of many books on the subjects of traction engines and tractors. Now Andrew takes us back to the beginning of the new pedigree with a pictorial review of the early development from one form of power to another. Journalist-historian Brian Crudge has been restoring tractors since 1972. Here he blocks in the background detail of the manufacturers, both sides of the Atlantic, who contributed their expertise and endeavour to the cause of tractor development.

The first farm vehicle successfully powered by a gasoline engine was built by an Iowa blacksmith, John Froehlich, in 1892. But the first commercially successful manufacturers were C. W. Hart and C. H. Parr of Charles City, Iowa, United States. Their No. 1 rolled off the production line in 1901. Now virtually indispensable to modern farmers, successive improvements in tractor design have greatly increased their efficiency and value. Unit construction pioneered by Henry Ford in 1917 stabilized production costs. Power-takeoff introduced in 1918, permitted direct transmission of power from the tractor engine to ancillary equipment, under the control of the tractor driver. The all-purpose, tricycle-type tractor of 1924 marked another advance. The year 1932 brought rubber tyres. Since 1954, more-versatile transmissions have been developed. Styling, as opposed to the purely functional engineering that characterized the early tractors, was adopted by manufacturers in the 1930s.

From 1918 the state of Nebraska decreed that the accuracy of claimed performance of tractors sold in that state must be tested by the University Engineering Department. The value to manufacturers of these tests has meant that tractor companies worldwide now use this service.

During World War 2, British Prime Minister Winston Churchill and American President Franklin D. Roosevelt, drafted the Lease-lend Bill under which, for the term of the emergency, Britain leased strategic military bases to the United States in return for the loan of destroyers and other equipment needed to boost the war effort, including vital agricultural machinery. It was due to this scheme that many British farmers remember with affection the older style American tractors they came to rely on during that period. In magnificent colour, Andrew has captured those thoroughbred tractors. He has tracked down, at local and national agricultural events, at museums, and in private collections in Britain and North America, lovingly restored tractors that bear witness to man's struggle to produce the perfect 'farmer's friend' — a mobile power pack at a competitive price which incidentally looks, smells and sounds great into the bargain.

Here then are the thoroughbreds — the historic tractors that bring a nostalgic gleam to the eye of enthusiasts all over the world, but particularly in their proving grounds of Britain and North America.

Right and Overleaf
Two views of the 1920 Advance-Rumely OilPull Model H, 16–30 drawbar-belt horsepower, serial number 5999, which has been restored by its owner George Bronson of Kalamazoo, Michigan. The traction engine pedigree is apparent, while the power unit is cross-mounted with direct drive to the wheels, and the large radiator uses oil for cooling purposes

Advance-Rumely

In 1889 the first practical tractor, produced by the Charter Gas Engine Company of Chicago, chugged into the field. It consisted of a single-cylinder gasoline engine mounted on a Rumely steam engine wheeled chassis. In 1909 the Advance-Rumely Company of Indiana began to explore the non-steam tractor business for itself with its OilPull range which included many traction engine features. Over 56,000 of these large machines were produced. By 1931 the design was becoming dated and the firm was taken over by Allis-Chalmers.

Albaugh-Dover

In 1916, Albaugh-Dover, a well-known American mailing house of Chicago, Illinois, took over the Kenney-Colwill Company of Norfolk, Nebraska. A year previously, Kenney-Colwill had announced the advent of a new tractor, the K.C. To exploit this new product, Albaugh-Dover set up the Square Turn Tractor Company in December 1917, first in Delaware, then back at Norfolk. Thus the K.C. or Square Turn tractor came into being, a front wheel drive unit with single rear wheel for steering, weighing over 3 tons, and powered by a Climax 4-cylinder 18–30, later 18–35 hp, engine. Its design remained basically unaltered until the company's assets were sold off in 1925.

The rare and still-worked Albaugh-Dover Square Turn owned by Kurt Umnus is shown at his farm, which hosts the North Central Steam and Gas Engine Club's annual event in August. The tractor has a unique system of fibre-faced cones enabling one front drive-wheel to travel forward, the other backward, so a sharp turn can be made

Allis-Chalmers

In business in America from 1901, Allis-Chalmers produced its first successful tractor, the 15–13, in 1918. Later Allis-Chalmers successfully adapted a design proposed by the short lived, Chicago based United Tractor and Implement Corporation, a consortium of which it was a member. From 1932 the Model U earned Allis-Chalmers tractors a reputation for good performance and reliability. Other types appeared including the Model B, originated in 1937, and its variants produced in Britain from 1948 until the late 1960s. Production then continued solely in America until Allis-Chalmers was taken over by Deutz in December 1985.

Well-known, popular – and temperamental – was the Allis-Chalmers B. This 1939 example is of American origin. From 1948, Model Bs with 16 hp engines were produced at Totton, near Southampton, England

Right
Allis-Chalmers G lightweight market-garden tractor of 1949, powered by a Continental engine. Nearly 30,000 units were manufactured from 1948 to 1955, but few were sold in Britain

Below
The Model L, produced from 1932, with 60–80 hp was the largest of the early crawlers. The original Continental engine was soon replaced by a 6-cylinder Allis-Chalmers engine with twin carburettors and exhausts

Made by the North Western Manufacturing Company of Milwaukee, this solid-tyred U28-3 of the 1930s, an industrial version of the Model U, is equipped with a mounted generator capable of producing 25 volts, 330 amps, supplied by the Hansen Arc Welder Company

Another popular model was the WC Rowcrop. Manufactured with a 24 hp engine at Milwaukee from 1933, in 1948 it was updated to become the WD. This model with V-twin front wheels dates from the mid-1940s

Below
Allis-Chalmers' best-known crawler in Britain, the Model M, was introduced in 1933. An agricultural model, it also saw much industrial use. This 1941 edition was photographed at the September 1988 Fovant Working, Wiltshire

Austin

Keen to provide British opposition to the Fordson F, in 1919 Herbert Austin produced his Model R. This rival design incorporated an Austin 20 hp car engine modified for unit construction (engine, gearbox and rear axle also forming the chassis) allied with Zenith carburettor for running on vaporising oil. Though successful in trials, it proved less reliable and more expensive than the Fordson, and even with a price reduction, did not enjoy large sales.

The Austin Model R at the Hunday Museum. All Austin tractor production was concentrated in France from 1927 until its end in 1932. A number of Austin tractors have been preserved, at least three in the west of England

Avery

In steam engine production from the late 1800s, the Avery Company made a none-too-successful venture into the internal combustion engine business in 1909. Continued attempts led to reasonable sales for this Peoria, Illinois, firm with the 20–35 in 1911, 12–25 in 1912 and 25–50 in 1914. Decline set in from 1923, the Company ceasing to trade in 1941. At one time R. A. Lister of Dursley, Gloucester was British agent for Avery.

The 40–80 was the largest tractor in the Avery range. Dating from 1913, its traction engine origin was obvious even though design was by now more styled. It was powered by a 4-cylinder engine made from two 2-cylinder 20–35 engines linked together. This impressive Avery is owned by Kurt Umnus of Wisconsin

Case

In 1892, the JI Case Threshing Machine Company of Racine, Wisconsin, made a brief entry into the tractor market with a large cross-motor machine. With demand for steam in decline, in 1910 Case re-entered the tractor market, still with cross-motor models. Competition forced the company to change to unit construction and longitudinal engine position with the Model L of 1929, while the DEX and other models came to Britain during the Second World War. Streamlining and a change of colour from grey to flambeau red gave sales a boost and production continued, Case becoming part of the Tenneco organisation in the 1970s.

Right
One of the first models to be introduced after 1910 was the 4-cylinder cross-motor 10–28. In 1928 it was updated as the Model A

Left
A close-up of this 1919 model owned and restored by John David of Maplewood, Ohio, reveals the compactness of the transverse engine mechanism

Fore and aft views show the design clearly, items of note being the front axle arrangement and extended rear wheel-strakes. The hand clutch was used on all Case models up to 1955

Rear-end view shows set-up for the driver, including easy access to implements for adjustment. Pictured at Prairieville Old Fashioned Farm Days, this Model L is owned by Nancy Thompson of Coldwater, Michigan

'Old Abe', the Case emblem, stands proud on this 4-cylinder 28–40 hp 1929 Model L, Case's first unit construction model. A self-starter was available from 1938, otherwise the model was little changed in 20 years

Carl Weismiller of Ithaca, Michigan is
the proud owner of this 1937 18 hp
Case RC with V-twin front wheels. A
wide front-axle rowcrop model was
also available

Above
This 1938 Case belongs to Betty and Lee Norton of Alto, Michigan

Left
Rear-end view of the Case R showing its low-slung and 'chunky' appearance, with adjustable hitch

The more successful Model S replaced the R in 1940, this one a 1942 SO orchard model. Owner Gene Webster is looking for the correct full-wings to complete its authentic restoration

Overleaf
The Case VAH 23 hp of 1948 is virtually unknown in Britain. An unusual high-clearance model, it was designed for use in the cotton and tobacco fields of Kentucky

Above
Tom Graverson uses his Case DC3 rowcrop for tractor pulling. He has uprated this 1942 45 hp model to 54 hp. Note the horn by the nearside rear wheel – to clear a space ahead?

Right
This larger 1952 DCS 'sugar cane special' gives a comparison of different styles of front axle on high-clearance models

Left
*A 1950 Case Model D ready to work
with Case Centinel 2 × 14 in bottom
plough. Owner Tom Graverson has
tuned this ex-Kentucky Parks
Department model to 45 hp*

Below
*This 1953 38 hp Case DC4 with rear-mounted 7 ft mower has an adjustable rear
axle for rowcrop working, but the more standard wide front axle*

Co-Op

The Duplex Machinery Company of Battle Creek, Michigan, in 1937 introduced three Co-op tractor models: No 1, a three-wheeled rowcrop with 4-cylinder Waukesha engine; No 2, a standard 4-wheeled model with 6-cylinder Chrysler engine, said to be capable of 28 mph; No 3, identical to No 2 but with a larger engine. From 1938 the manufacturer became known as the Co-operative Manufacturing Company, while from 1940 the models were produced by the Arthurdale Farm Equipment Corporation, West Virginia, the run ending not long afterwards.

Right
This Co-op B2JR of 1941, serial number 178, manufactured in Shelbyville, Indiana, is owned by Lavon Fred of Fred Farms, Rochester, Indiana

Below
Another view of the Co-op, possibly an updated No 2 rowcrop version with wide rear axle and 'tip-toe' front wheels

David Brown

Well known for gears and Aston Martin cars, the David Brown
Company of Huddersfield, Yorkshire, produced a Model A
tractor for Ferguson in 1936, followed by its own Model VAK I
in 1939. This was improved to become the VAK IA in 1945,
then the Cropmaster in 1947, taking David Brown into the
diesel era by 1952, with industrials and tracked machines too.
Production continued throughout the fifties and sixties,
David Brown becoming, with Case, part of the Tenneco
organisation of America in 1972.

*Our one example is a VAK IA of 1946 with 4-cylinder 35 hp petrol/T.V.O. engine.
Under three different owners in preservation, this tractor has worked hard at
many events in the Yeovil and Crewkerne areas of Somerset*

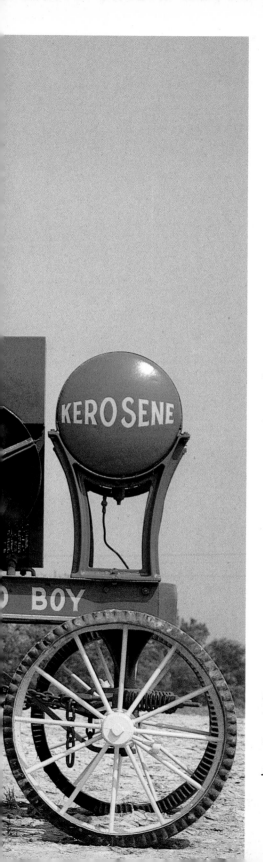

John Deere

The Waterloo Boy, known in Britain as the Overtime, was the progeny of the Waterloo Gasoline Engine Company of Waterloo, Iowa. It appeared in 1912. Following a take-over, the company adopted the name John Deere. The first 'real' John Deere was the renowned Model D, in production from 1923 until 1952, the longest run of any tractor model. Two-cylinder horizontal engines were used for all tractors right up to 1962, including, from 1949, a diesel version. John Deere retains an important position in the present day tractor market.

Known as the Model N from 1915, the Waterloo Boy was a popular tractor of 12–25 hp with two forward, one reverse gears. This model dates from 1919, a year after the take-over by John Deere

Still retaining a little of the traction engine influence in open gearing and steering system, production of this 'giant in power, miser in fuel' ceased in 1924. Owned by Phil Welsh of Alloga, Michigan, it is pictured at an event in Benton, in the state of Michigan

*Jeff Wilson and son Troy are proud
owners of this 1941 Model A, the 30 hp
big sister of the Model B. The three-
wheeled version was designated
the AN*

Introduced in 1933, the John Deere Model A continued in production to 1947. This rear view shows the tractor, complete with spade-lug wheels, after a hard day's work

This low-slung model, the orchard version of the A, though late in the series, is unstyled. It is owned by Betty Norton of Michigan

A close-up shows the 2-cylinder horizontal engine of this 1946 John Deere, Model AO, serial number 266146, 20.35 drawbar, 26.30 belt horsepower

Engineered in the early 1930s, the Model AW was styled in 1936. This standard rowcrop with French and Hecht spoked wheels, shows the typical John Deere steering and full-view driver's position

Overleaf
This 20 hp John Deere BW with unusual wheels dates from the late 1930s. It is shown cultivating at Fovant in Wiltshire, UK. The complicated set-up for rear and mid-mounted implements must have made the advent of the hydraulic system quite a relief

Left

The Model B of 1935 was a one-plow tractor of only 9 hp, but through its term of production to 1952 many improvements were made, including engine uprating to 24 hp and 6-speed gearbox. This unit dates from 1941

Left below

The year 1937 saw the introduction of John Deere's largest rowcrop tractor, the 35 hp Model G. This 1953 model is owned by Maurice Horn of Rochester, Indiana

Right

A front view confirms it to be a high-crop

Above
The John Deere Model G standard
rowcrop was produced 1943–53, the
lighting being an extra. The flywheel
positioned by the nearside wheel was
turned under decompression for
starting, though from 1947 some
models had electric starting

Left
In 1953 the 60, a model with a pressed type frame as opposed to earlier cast
frame design, replaced the B. In 1956 the 60 gave place to the 620

Fowler

Best-known for steam ploughing engines in the 1920s, the UK-based firm John Fowler of Leeds successfully challenged more-established suppliers with its range of motorised ploughs and crawlers. In 1927 Fowler patented the Gyrotiller. Becoming with Marshall part of the Thomas Ward Group in 1947, the renowned VF crawler with Marshall 40 hp single-cylinder engine was developed. This was superseded in due course by the Challenger series of crawlers.

The complete machine, one of the larger 150–180 hp units of the late 1930s pictured at the Hunday Museum. The arrow indicates to the driver the position of the front wheel, used for steering

Frick

Today a leader in the refrigeration business, the Frick
Company was set up at Waynesboro, Pennsylvania in 1853,
becoming well-known for threshers, steam engines and
sawmills too. In 1913 the company, while selling tractors for
the Ohio Tractor Company, began working on its own Model
A of around two-and-a-half tons with 4-cylinder overhead
valve Erd 12–20 hp engine and two-forward, one reverse,
gears. Available for ten years from 1918, in 1921 Model A was
joined by the 15–28 hp Model B with 4-cylinder Beaver engine,
roller bearings and improved air-cleaner design. Its own
tractor production ceasing in 1928, the Frick Company sold
Minneapolis tractors for two years before concentrating
solely on refrigeration.

*Pictured at Rollag, the unusual design of the Frick tractor is apparent. In keeping
with some other companies of that era, Frick favoured large diameter front
wheels, the theory being that there was less bearing wear, less soil compaction
and less power needed for running over uneven ground*

Friday

In 1948 the Friday Tractor Company of Hartford, Michigan entered the tractor market with its 3-plow Model 0-48 intended mainly for orchard use or delivering produce to market. With 6-cylinder Chrysler engine, Dodge 5-speed gearbox, 2-speed rear axle and electric starting, this one-and-a-half ton model continued in production until the late 1950s.

Small but sleek and powerful, this Friday looks more modern than 1949. Who would guess 90 hp lurked under the bonnet? It can reach a speed of 60 mph! Number 5009, pictured at the Van Buren Flywheelers meeting, is owned by Larry Darling of Hartford, Michigan

Graham-Bradley

Already building cars, the Graham-Paige Motors Corporation of Detroit, Michigan, in the late 1930s introduced two tractor models to their range: in 1938, the Graham-Bradley 32 hp rowcrop model, and in 1939 the Graham-Bradley Model 104, a standard version of the earlier model with 6-cylinder engine and speeds from 2 to 20 mph. Production ceased in 1945 and though a new line was announced in 1946, this was shelved in favour of car production.

The 1938 Graham-Bradley 32 hp tractor, weighing about one-and-a-half tons and powered by a 6-cylinder Graham-Paige $3\frac{1}{4}$ in bore × $4\frac{3}{8}$ in stroke car engine, is seen here at Jim Monaghan's Antique Engine Show, Michigan

Howard

A. C. 'Cliff' Howard, having designed a powered rotary cultivator with 60 hp Buda engine in 1920, set up Austral Auto Cultivators in 1922. He opened a factory in Northmead, New South Wales, Australia. Here for the next 20 years the 22 hp DH22 was produced. Only minor improvements, like rubber-tyred wheels and power lift for the rotary cultivators, proved necessary. Two models were available: standard for orchard and field work and a sugar cane version for deep-working, both very successful. A range of crawlers became available from 1952, but the world-wide company concentrated on implements like the tractor-mounted and well known Howard Rotavator. A. C. Howard died in England in 1971. The company continues today.

Produced from 1928, the Howard DH22 had a 22 hp overhead valve engine and magneto ignition. The power unit could be separated from the culvitator and used to some extent as a tractor. Other attachments were considered but apparently not produced. This example, rare in Britain, is pictured at the Hunday Museum

Huber

An early 1900s' Huber pictured at Rollag, demonstrates the massive design and its traction engine pedigree. Hopefully, the extra wide rear wheels would prevent the huge machine's sinking in soft earth

Firmly established at Marion, Ohio, USA in the 1863–98 period, the Huber Manufacturing Company made everything from hayrakes to steam engines for agriculture. In 1894 Huber took over Van Duzen, a company which had recently built a tractor. Four years later Huber introduced a hybrid with Van Duzen internal-combustion engine and Huber traction engine transmission. Thirty units were produced that year. Huber became the first company to have a production run. Soon after, however, Huber left the tractor

Below
A close-up of the Waukesha 4-cylinder cross-mounted engine of 15–30 hp, increased to 18–36 in 1925, the last year of production

Right
Exhibited in its correct nut-brown livery at the Van Buren Flywheelers event, is the updated Super Four owned by Cliff Peterson of Grass Lake, Michigan

business, to reappear in 1911 with the 13–22 hp 'Farmer's Tractor' range. Huber made its name with its Light Four tractors produced from 1917 to 1925. Re-designed Super Four models appeared in 1926 followed by the 'Modern Farmer' range of standard, rowcrop and orchard models. The forty-year tractor run ended prior to the Second World War, but Huber remains in business manufacturing construction equipment.

Right below
This view from the other side of Cliff's Super Four shows the large front wheels which were used by other companies, like Frick, also during that period

A change of colour and design are
discernable in these two examples
from the Huber Super Four range of 18
hp upwards, which enjoyed a 13-year
production run from 1926.
Photographed at Rollag, the rear
model has spade-lugs fitted for extra
wheel grip

International

Following the merging of several companies including McCormick and Deering, the International Harvester Company of Chicago, Illinois, was born in 1902. Series tractor production began with the Mogul (1914) and Titan (1915). These were replaced in 1923 by the McCormick-Deering Farmall range 10–20, one of the first tractors designed with a one-piece cast-iron frame. In 1939 came a change of colour, style and design with the International Farmall A, M and H rowcrop models among others, plus the W4, 6 and 9 standard series. Crawlers, UK production and diesel traction were introduced from the 1940s onwards, plus a selection of agricultural models including the 1956 B250, the first completely British-designed model. International Harvester production continues, but since 1985 under the Tenneco banner with Case and David Brown.

Built in thousands from 1923 to 1939 the McCormick-Deering 10–20 pictured here at Kurt Umnus's farm is one of the best known of the Farmall range. French and Hecht spoked wheels were used in America, solid Dunlop centres in Britain. This model has an extended air-stack more usually associated with the W30

'As broad as it is long', this 20 hp F20 has a mere 8-foot turning radius and high-speed road gearbox providing 18 mph. This model restored by Steve Wade of Plainwell, Michigan, is pictured at Prairieville Old Fashioned Farm Days

The view from the rear of this 1934 F20 suggests the high-road speed was quite an experience. Introduced in 1924, the F20 was the original Farmall and rowcrop tractor model, offered with implements designed to fit on its frame – power-lift an optional extra

Previous page
The McCormick-Deering/International W12 was the standard version of the rowcrop 16 hp F12, produced from 1934 to 1938, then in 1939 it was produced with 18 hp engine and redesignated the W140. This model of 1934 vintage is owned by Stewart Webster of Kalamazoo, Michigan

The rowcrop F30 was built from 1931
with 4-cylinder 30 hp engine and 4-
speed gearbox. Standard (W30) and
industrial models became available
from 1932. This 1937 F30 was restored
by Eugene Wahl

Below
Farmall F30 in close-up. From 1939
this tractor was to become the basis of
the 'new' Farmall M, one of the best-
known farm tractors in America

Farmall 'super-power' working at
Fovant, the BMD assisting one of the
W range in hauling a heavy set of
rollers. Built at Doncaster, UK, the
Farmall M became the BM, then, with
50 hp diesel engine and option of
swinging drawbar and hydraulic lift,
in 1952 it became the BMD (British –
Model M – Diesel)

Popular for ploughing, but
comparatively rarely seen preserved
in Britain, is the 24 hp W4. Introduced
in 1940 it was designed with cast
frame, 5-speed gearbox, independent
brakes and other useful features.
Together with the larger W6 and W9
it came to Britain under the wartime
Lease-Lend scheme

Ivel

Dan Albone of Biggleswade, Bedfordshire transferred his salesmanship and engineering expertise from bicycles to tractors and by 1902 he had produced his revolutionary Ivel, named after the nearby river. Up to that date tractors had been based on steam traction engine design and were relatively clumsy compared with this 2-cylinder 10/22 hp model weighing less than two tons. Using an engine supplied by a Coventry firm, production began in 1903. A year later the forward gears were doubled to two and by 1920, 980 units had been produced. Engine covers were available but were seldom used and soon lost. Sadly, Dan Albone died in 1906, and without his drive and dedication, by 1916 the design had become dated and the firm went out of production.

Right
The side view of this 1903–4 model shows the girder chassis, tidy power unit and cable steering. Photographed at the Hunday Museum, it is one of only two known Ivels of this vintage surviving in Britain, the other being at the Science Museum, London

Left
Not often pictured, the rear view shows the fuel tank under the driver's seat and beside it the 30-gallon water tank (there was no radiator) used for cooling and ballast purposes. The 'chimney' above it is the air vent. Solid tyres are a recent addition to prolong the wheel-life of this still-used, unique machine

Marshall

With single-cylinder design dated, the MP6 with conventional Leyland 350 6-cylinder 70 hp diesel engine was planned in 1954, ready for sale by 1957. Sadly, the British farmer was not ready for such a machine, but a reasonable number were exported. This MP6 is pictured at the Great Dorset Steam Fair

With steam sales declining and impressed by the simplicity of Germany's Lanz diesel tractor design, Marshall of Gainsborough, Lincolnshire, decided to explore the Lanz concept in preference to its own ungainly 1907 tractor. Thus in 1930 the 15–30 was born introducing the single-cylinder two-stroke horizontal diesel engine that was to become the Marshall hallmark through Marshall M, Field Marshall Series 1, 2 and 3, and finally 3A, ending in 1957. In the meantime Track-Marshall machines developed the crawler side of the business.

The 40 hp Field Marshall Series I followed the 20 hp Model M in 1945; Series 2 from 1947. This Series 2 close-up shows the Field Marshall logo, plus belt pulley which incorporated the clutch mechanism

The independent brake levers on the Series 2 can be seen adjacent to the mudguards of this 1947 contractor's model with 9 mph top speed (6 mph on others). The pulley to the left of the exhaust powers the dynamo for the lighting system

The lighting equipment can be clearly seen on this Marshall Series 3A, the final development of the single-cylinder concept. A colour change to orange, plus extras like electric starting and rear lift for implements, failed to reverse the market turned away from single-cylinder design. Production ceased in 1957

Massey-Harris 101 Super came into being a year after introduction in 1939 as the 101, the first model to dispense with the original Wallis U-shaped boiler-plate frame concept. Number 259643 of 1941, driven by Lavon Fred, is owned by Scott Fred of Fred Farms, Indiana

Massey-Harris

Formed by the merger of two companies in 1891, Massey-Harris of Toronto, Canada, continued selling farm implements. From 1917, Bull and Parrett tractors were added to its range of merchandise. Purchase of the J. I. Case Plow Works in 1928 enabled Massey-Harris to produce Wallis tractors, selling the rights to the Case name to the J. I. Case Threshing Machine Company. Its own M-H 15–22 General Purpose 4-wheel-drive tractor of 1936 was not a great success, but the company fared better in adapting the 1929 Wallis 12–20 as the basis for its Pacemaker and Challenger models that same year. Expansion continued, purchase of F. Perkins of Peterborough, Cambridgeshire, in 1958 giving the company its own source of diesel engines. Five years earlier, in 1953, merger with Ferguson saw the conglomerate become Massey-Ferguson which is still producing tractors today.

The first Massey-Harris true rowcrop tractor, the Challenger, was produced from 1936 to 1939. This model, owned by the Petersons of Chesterton, Indiana and photographed at Domino's Farms, shows the original livery. Later models were red and cream. Though a popular tractor its 16/27 hp engine was not noted for reliability, causing the firm to look outside for power units for a time

The M-H 101 Super was powered by a
Continental side-valve engine of
26–40 hp from six cylinders, though
some of the early machines had
Chrysler engines. Production ceased
in 1946

Above

Prior to the Ferguson merger, the 16–27 hp M-H Pony was the firm's smallest, yet best-selling tractor, popular on smaller farms. In production from 1947 to 1952 with another short run in 1957, the Pony had a 4-cylinder Continental engine, plus, from 1950, hydraulic lift. This 1951 model is owned by Larry Darling of Michigan

Minneapolis-Moline

In 1929 the Minneapolis Threshing Machine Company (Minneapolis tractors), the Minneapolis Steel & Machinery Company (Twin-City tractors) and the Moline Plow Company (Moline tractors and implements) merged to form the Minneapolis Power Implement Company for strength in difficult times. The Twin City name was used while production was streamlined, the new M-M range appearing from 1930. Some models were exported to Britain in wartime where UDS models were built until MM (England) went into receivership in 1949. American production continued and the Avery Company was taken over, MM itself becoming part of the White Corporation in 1963, joining Oliver and Cockshutt. In 1972 production was transferred from Minneapolis, Minnesota to Charles City, Iowa. By 1974 the MM name had disappeared from tractors in favour of White.

At 12½ tons the 60–90 was the biggest tractor on the prairies. It was of similar design to the Twin City 40 – just bigger. Engine cylinder size was also the same, but the number increased to six to guarantee the 90 hp. This machine received excellent reviews

One of a series of photographs taken at Rollag shows a Twin City 40 hp decal. This appeared on models built from 1910 to the time of merger. Twin City tractors' pioneering design of exposed engine, cylindrical radiator and canopy influenced tractor production for the next ten years

Right
The 60–90 was produced from 1913 to 1920, with radiator capacity of 116 gallons, fuel tank 95 gallons and the single-speed gearbox driving the 7-feet diameter wheels a maximum 2 mph. As with other models, the engine was cranked from the driver's platform for starting

Below right
A close-up of the unusual engine design: the 40 hp coming from four separate cylinders with overhead valves. In one test the engine was calculated to have developed nearly 50 hp

Left
*Following a Nebraska Test in 1920,
the 40–80 model which had been
introduced by the Minneapolis
Threshing Machine Company in 1912,
was re-rated a 35–70. Although the
tractor had a radiator, water capacity
was as much as 50 gallons*

Below left
*An example of the Minneapolis-Moline
Standard J on offer from 1936 to 1938,
the Universal J being the rowcrop
version. Both had 4-cylinder engines
and 5-speed 2–12 mph gearboxes. The
air-cleaner stack on this design would
seem to be in a precarious position*

The Minneapolis 17–30 by the same company came out in 1922 with 4-cylinder cross-engine still allowing direct drive through simple gearing. A useful feature was removable cylinder sleeves to assist engine repair. Like the 35–70, this model was available until the 1929 merger

Above

A 27.09 hp example of the M-M Model R range at Domino's Farm. The R series were the smallest of the M-M range, available in England and America from 1939. This is an RTU with twin front wheels, the standard model being RTS and the single-front-wheel rowcrop model, RTN

Left

A M-M UDLX, based on the well-known Model U, at Rollag. To make the driver's life easier, not only cab but upholstered seats, electric clock, heater and many other items including speed up to 40 mph were available, but the model was too far ahead of its time and too expensive. In two years of production less than 150 sold

A M-M 36.3 hp Jeep with owner-restorer Ernest Weissert at the wheel. Military vehicles, originally tractor conversions, were produced from 1938, a number being assigned to the Minnesota National Guard in 1940. A guardsman dubbed the unit a 'Jeep' after a character in the Popeye cartoons, and so the name stuck

*Rear view of model NTX 4 × 4 Jeep of
1944, powered by a 'Z' tractor engine,
in its correct Navy green complete
with Navy number*

The Model Z was one of the second batch of tractor models produced by Minneapolis-Moline after the 1929 merger. Introduced in 1939, it boasted streamlined hood, electric lights and fenders or mudguards among its new features. During wartime, models were available in Britain. The engine used was similar to that of the Model R, early units having the means of altering the compression to suit prevailing conditions

From 1949 the Model Z was uprated to become the ZA. Ernest Weissert's 36.2 hp tractor is an example. Available with 5-speed gearbox throughout the range, Z production in its various forms ended in 1953

Above
In 1947 the M-M GTA was updated to become the Model G. This 70.6 hp example runs on liquid propane gas (LPG) which was used to fuel a number of farm tractors from the 1930s

Below right
The normal fuel tank was replaced by a refillable LPG storage tank neatly incorporated into the general design. The other necessary fitments can also be seen on this model from Ernest Weissert's collection

In 1939 Cletrac produced its own
wheeled tractor, the tricycle-style
General GG, taken over by BF Avery of
Louisville, Kentucky and uprated to
become their 19 hp Model A. Avery
also produced a smaller Hercules-
engined Model V shown here, which
M-M kept in production when it took
over Avery in 1944

Oliver

From 1901 Charles Hart and Charles Parr of Iowa combined their talents to produce the large Hart-Parr tractors. In 1929 they merged with the Oliver Chilled Plow Company and others to become the Oliver Corporation. Oliver Hart-Parr tractors were produced. From 1937 Hart-Parr was dropped from the name plate. The Cleveland Tractor Company, maker of Cletrac, was absorbed by Oliver in 1944 and crawler production continued to 1960. After the end of the wartime Lease-Lend scheme under which the Oliver 80 was imported, no more Oliver tractors came to the United Kingdom, though some were manufactured in Britain by David Brown from 1960. Together with Minneapolis-Moline and Cockshutt who sold Oliver tractors under their own name, Oliver became part of the White Motor Corporation in 1962.

An Oliver Hart-Parr 28-44 of 1936, owned by G. Mitchell of Fulton, Michigan. Built from 1930 to 1937, this 4-cylinder model was one of the first produced following the 1929 merger. The industrial version was the first Oliver to run on pneumatic tyres

Right
The Oliver 70, originally Oliver Hart-Parr 70, was offered from 1935 to 1937. An improved version was available right up to 1948, with a smooth-running 6-cylinder 23/28 hp engine. Optional equipment included battery, electric starter and lights. Standard and industrial versions were available in addition to this 1938 rowcrop model owned by Frank Mitchell

Below right
Produced from 1940 to 1948, the streamlined 16.5 hp Oliver 60 was a popular tractor and many survive in America. The V-twin front end is clearly seen on this 1947 model

Another view of the standard Oliver 60, its $3\frac{1}{2}$ in bore $\times$ $3\frac{5}{16}$ in stroke 4-cylinder engine hidden by the side-plates for the fully streamlined effect popular among firms of that era. Whether the side-plates always remained in position when working is open to question

Previous page
Like many other firms Oliver produced different versions of each model according to the use required. This 1945 Oliver 60 is the standard version with a wide front axle

This front-end shot of the same tractor affords interesting comparison between the chassis fitting for the wide-axle Oliver 60 and that for the V-twin 60 pictured earlier

The rowcrop Oliver 80 was a development of the 18-27 rowcrop of the 1930s. It had one more forward gear than the standard model, and a 4-cylinder 25–40 hp engine. This is a 1940 model

Inset left
A more rugged looking tractor than the styled 60 and 70, the 80 was the best known Oliver in Britain, imported by the War Agricultural Committee on the Lease-Lend scheme. Its production run was from 1937 to 1948. The fine collection of Oliver tractors owned by the Mitchell brothers was photographed at Prairieville Old Fashioned Farm Days

Below right
Better-known in the UK for ploughs, Cockshutt sold Oliver tractors under its own name in Canada, then from 1946 produced its own models, the parts for these virtually all bought in. The 1951 Cockshutt 50 illustrated here was the largest in the range, powered by a 6-cylinder Buda engine and showing its Oliver pedigree

The Oliver 'Super' series had a four-year production run from 1954. This Oliver Super 55, 30/34 hp of 1957 belongs to Morrie Pitlick of Oxford, Iowa. Special features include independent power-takeoff, hydraulics, independent disc brakes and optional 3-point hitch

Right
Another example is the 1957, 37 drawbar hp Super 77, again owned by Morrie Pitlick and photographed at the World Plowing Championships in Iowa. Other Super models were 66, 88 and 99, and a choice of petrol or diesel engines was available. The 'cab' on this one was not supplied as standard

Rushton

While working for the Associated Engineering Company (AEC), George Rushton developed the General, a British tractor to compete with the Fordson. The first model appeared in 1928, a modified Fordson incorporating Rushton's patents. In 1929 a separate company was set up in the old AEC works at Walthamstow, London, the tractor now titled the Rushton. In addition to agricultural models, industrials and others were built. Improvements were made, but with Fordson now in production at Dagenham, competition was too great and Rushton went out of business in the mid-1930s.

This well-restored Rushton of the 1930s resides at the Hunday Museum. Powered by a 4-cylinder 14/20 hp engine, the Rushton did well in trials, but farmers preferred the less expensive Fordson or other established makes. Nevertheless, the Rushton played a significant part in British tractor history

Silver King

In 1933 the Fate-Root-Heath Company of Plymouth, Massachusetts, launched a Hercules-engined tractor weighing less than a ton and offering a top-speed of 20 mph. It was named the Plymouth 10-20. In 1935 it was renamed the Silver King R38. The first Silver King tricycle model appeared in 1936, powered by a 4-cylinder Hercules IXA engine of 16 hp. It was followed in 1940 by the updated 600, 660 and 700 models with Continental engines and speeds of up to 30 mph. Four-wheel models with electric starting, lighting and other features were produced. In 1956 Silver King production transferred to Clarksburg, West Virginia. Two years later the brand name disappeared from the tractor market.

'A thing of beauty is a joy forever' (John Keats). The Silver King did look impressive. It had a reasonable production run and all its features were kept up-to-date, influenced by car design. This model is owned by Alton Schwark of Washington, and was photographed at Domino's Farms

Built by Fate-Root-Heath this 1940s Silver King is powered by a Hercules IXB, $3\frac{1}{4}$ in bore $\times$ 4 in stroke engine

Turner

In 1945 the gearbox makers Turner of Wolverhampton announced the company's intention to build a new tractor. Appearing two years later the new model was named Yeoman of England. The engine chosen was a V-twin diesel, already used by Turner for industrial and marine purposes. Building on earlier success with the Fowler Company, skilled diesel engineer Freeman Saunders had opened his own small engineering business in Cornwall. He was employed by Turner to deal with early problems in their design. Although most of the gremlins had been exorcised by 1951, the Yeoman remained an expensive machine in comparison with other established makes. The tractor did not achieve high sales.

Looking impressive, the 34—40 hp 1948 Turner 'Yeoman of England' is pictured at Stourpaine. One of the pair of cylinder banks of the V-twin 4-cylinder diesel engine can be clearly seen. The tractor found its best use with contractors, but sadly could not compete with already established makes in price or performance